MEGATECH

Cyber Space

Virtual reality and the World Wide Web

David Jefferis

Crabtree

Introduction

Welcome to cyberspace, the area of electronic communications made possible by computer technology.

Today, people across the world can be 'connected,' or wired together, by the Internet, a system that puts computer users in direct contact with each other and with services and companies. Through the Internet, anyone with a desktop computer can be a part of the connected 'world community'.

Cyberspace allows people who are 'hooked up' by computer to send and receive information quickly and easily.

Crabtree Publishing Company

PMB 16A
350 Fifth Ave
Ste. 3308
New York
NY 10118

612 Welland Ave
St. Catharines, ON
Canada L2M 5V6

Edited by
Norman Barrett
Coordinating editor
Ellen Rodger
Consulting editor
Virginia Mainprize

Technical consultant
Mat Irvine FBIS

Picture research by
David Pratt
Created and produced by
Alpha Communications in association
with Firecrest Books Ltd.

©1999 Alpha Communications and
©1999 Firecrest Books Ltd.

Cataloging-in-Publication Data
Jefferis, David.
    Cyber space: virtual reality and the
World Wide Web / David Jefferis;
technical consultant, Mat Irvine.
    p. cm. -- (Megatech)
    Includes index.
    Summary: Surveys digital
technology from the early days of
computers to virtual reality and the
World Wide Web, describing the uses of
computer simulation in flight, battle,
hazardous environments, and
entertainment.
ISBN 0-7787-0057-7 (paper). --
ISBN 0-7787-0047-X (rlb)
    1. Computers--History--Juvenile
literature. 2. Computer simulation--
Juvenile literature. 3. Virtual reality--
Juvenile literature. 4. World Wide Web
(Information retrieval system)--
Juvenile literature. [1. Computers. 2.
Computer simulation. 3. Virtual
reality.] I. Irvine, Mat. II. Title. III.
Series.
QA76.23.J44 1999
004--dc21 LC 98-48512
CIP AC

Pictures on these pages, clockwise
from far left:
1 Virtual reality headset and dataglove.
2 Graphic impression of cyberspace
connections of a city.
3 Computer rendering of a face.
4 Controller in airborne post.
5 CGI raptor dinosaur.
6 CGI 'wireframe' image.
Previous page:
Technician works with virtual reality.

Color separation by
Job Color, Italy
Printed in Spain by
GZ Printek

Contents

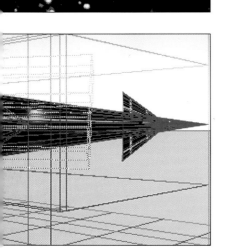

Exploring cyberspace

▲ *Many modern cities all over the world have electronic communications links in banks, shops, homes, and even taxis.*

Cyberspace is a word used for the great electronic 'universe' that opened up when computer technology linked with advanced communications.

▶ *A researcher wears a headset to view a world created by computer. This electronic environment is known as virtual reality.*

Cyberspace refers to the system of computer networks that link computer users all over the world. In cyberspace, sounds and pictures may be of real things, such as a space probe view of Mars or a medical image inside a person's body. Cyberspace also includes the area of 'virtual reality,' where images of people or events are created by a computer and seem to duplicate the real thing.

◀ *Cyberspace makes remote-control operation of equipment possible for all sorts of jobs, from underwater exploring, such as this probe of the future, to inspecting oil pipelines.*

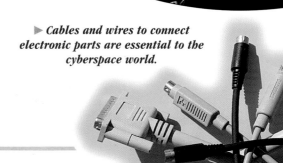

▶ *Cables and wires to connect electronic parts are essential to the cyberspace world.*

◀ *Fighting wars has become a cyberspace activity. Crew members aboard a flying command post detect enemy air, ground, and sea movements.*

The word 'cyberspace' was first used by science-fiction author William Gibson in his 1984 novel, Neuromancer. In the book, people connect their brains directly to computer networks where information appears visually. They travel in the electronic world as if it were a real place.

The 'cyber' part of the term cyberspace is older and was taken from cybernetics, a word coined in 1948 to describe the science of automatic control and communication systems, especially in robots and electronics. The term comes from kubernetes, an ancient Greek word for steersman or navigator.

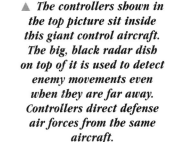

▲ *The controllers shown in the top picture sit inside this giant control aircraft. The big, black radar dish on top of it is used to detect enemy movements even when they are far away. Controllers direct defense air forces from the same aircraft.*

What is the information superhighway?

???

The information superhighway is the 'connected' world, where everyone is linked by electronic communications.

The most efficient computer information-carriers today are optical fibers. These are extremely fine strands of bendable plastic that carry light through their hollow insides. By converting computer signals from rapid-fire electric pulses to flashes of light, optical fibers are used for sending information.

Optical fibers can carry thousands of times as much information as old-fashioned wires and cables, which is why the system is called the 'superhighway'. It is also known as the 'digital highway', because a digital code is used by all of today's electronic equipment. You can find out more about this network on page 8.

Today, anyone with a home computer can enter cyberspace by using the worldwide connections of the Internet system. With this electronic 'spider's web', distance has little meaning. You can communicate as easily with a person in a far-distant continent as you can with someone just around the corner.

Telecom revolution

▲ Radio antennas beam messages almost instantly.

Before the age of long-distance telecommunications, the quickest way to send a message was on horseback. In the 1830s, that changed with the invention of the electric telegraph, which sent messages at high speed along a wire.

▲ Before the electric telegraph, semaphore was often used to send signals. In France, Claude Chappe developed a system of over 500 semaphore stations, each with mechanical signal arms.

The electric telegraph was developed by engineers in the United States and Britain. Messages were sent by operators as coded electrical signals through wires that joined sending and receiving stations. The operators used the Morse code, a system that used combinations of dots and dashes instead of letters and numbers.

In 1876, inventor Alexander Graham Bell developed the telephone, which let people speak over the wires. This new invention was a great success. In 1880, there were just 33,000 telephones in the world. Ten years later, there were nearly half a million.

▶ Use of the telephone grew fast, much like the Internet today. In the 1980s, radio-based mobile telephones were developed, and many homes now have them. An airline trip once meant being out of touch. That changed in 1995, when telephones were installed in the seat armrests of Kuwait Airways jets.

▲ This radio dates from the 1920s, when music and drama programs were very popular.

In 1887, German scientist Heinrich Hertz proved the existence of invisible radio waves that moved at the speed of light, 186,000 miles per second (300,000 km/sec). By 1894, Italian Guglielmo Marconi had invented the 'wireless telegraph.' In 1901, he successfully sent a radio signal across the Atlantic Ocean, from Britain to Canada.

The first television broadcasts were made in the 1930s, but the cyberspace world of telecommunications had to wait until the development of small, fast, and reliable computers.

▲ *ENIAC was built in 1946. It used a digital program but operated using electrons that flowed in non-digital valves. Although massive, ENIAC had less computing power than a pocket calculator.*

▶ *Today's equipment is based on the calculating power of the integrated circuit. The one shown here is a Pentium chip, used in millions of desktop computers worldwide.*

Early computers, first developed to crack secret codes during World War II, were very large and had many unreliable parts. However, the 'microchip', developed in 1959, changed things dramatically. Electronic parts were now packed together as an 'integrated circuit' on a tiny chip of silicon. As a result, all electronic machines could be made smaller, cheaper, faster, and more reliable.

The final key to cyberspace was 'digitization.' Digitization involves changing information into a digital code that can be sent quickly between computers. Computers are digital machines. They work through programs that use a binary code (just two numbers, which represent 'on' and 'off') for all tasks, such as simple calculating, word processing, or sending and receiving Internet messages.

▼ *All information is digitized, broken down into a series of 'on' or 'off' electronic signals.*

Enlarged view of circled part of picture at left

DIGITAL CODE

Computers use the digital system, a simple 'binary' code that works by using just two figures, or digits — 1 (one) and 0 (zero).

These digits represent 'on' and 'off' as electric pulses racing around inside a computer. Any information can be converted ('digitized') into a series of these on-off electric signals, to be used within a computer to solve a problem, or send signals very quickly to another computer.

Because of the speed and simplicity of communications using digital equipment, the computer has become the basic tool of the cyberspace universe.

Birth of the Internet

◀ *Technology that makes the Net possible: designing a computer chip.*

The Internet (or 'Net') is a system that links millions of computers together. Anyone who works on a computer that is linked to the Net can use it for research and communication.

A huge advantage of the Internet over many other computer linkups is that special software allows communications between different types of computers. Users can exchange information wherever they are.

▶ *Fear of nuclear attack led planners to design a communication system that was not centralized. If parts were destroyed, messages could still get through on an undamaged route.*

What is e-mail?

E-mail is short for electronic mail, the standard way of sending messages on the Internet.

To use e-mail, you type out a message on your computer keyboard in an e-mail program and then transmit it to the Internet.

It goes to the electronic address you give it, just like a pen-and-paper letter, or 'snail mail', goes to the address on the envelope. At the other end, the e-mail is received by a central computer which acts as a kind of post office box. When the recipient calls up his or her e-mail, it can then be opened and read, like any other computer document.

E-mail is often a time-saver, as you can type out several notes, then send them all at once. They take only a few seconds to be transmitted.

The Internet was developed because of the 'cold war,' a power struggle between communist and non-communist countries that lasted from 1945 to 1989. In the early 1950s, the United States defense planners were concerned about what would happen if Soviet nuclear weapons destroyed key parts of the United States' communications system. They asked questions such as: What if the U.S. president could not order a counter-strike? One solution was a system that was not centralized, so that even if parts of it were destroyed, messages could still get through on other routes.

This first Internet, named the ARPAnet, was set up in the 1960s. It provided a safe way for the government and the military to talk to each other. Soon, many defense researchers and universities (who often carry out military research) were linked up. From then on, there was no stopping the growth of the Net.

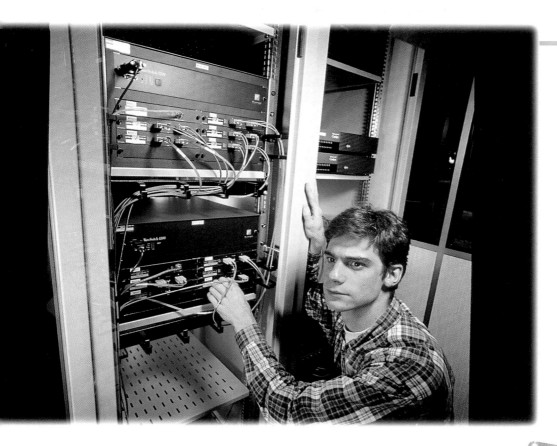

▲ *Ray Tomlinson devised the electronic mail system in the U.S. in 1972. He used the now-universal 'at' symbol to show an e-mail address : this person @ that computer.*

◄ *Big and powerful host server computers are used to maintain permanent connections to the Internet. Through these, users can go online anytime.*

The Internet uses many powerful 'server' computers, all interconnected to control the flow of information. In 1999, there were about 10 million 'server' computers. Signals pass through the system at about 186,000 mph (300,000 km/sec).

To access this network you 'dial up' to a server using your own computer and telephone line. Once you are connected, or 'online', messages pass around the Net in the quickest way possible. The first available route may be close by or far away, but distance makes little difference to the time it takes to complete the link.

JARGON EXPLAINED
Here are some of the tongue-twister terms that have come into common use in the Internet system.

FTP File Transfer Protocol. Software that allows computers of any type to communicate and transfer text files across the Net.

IP Internet Protocol. Just as every telephone has its own number, every computer connected to the Internet has an Internet protocol number.

Host server 'Gateway' computer that joins individual machines to the Internet.

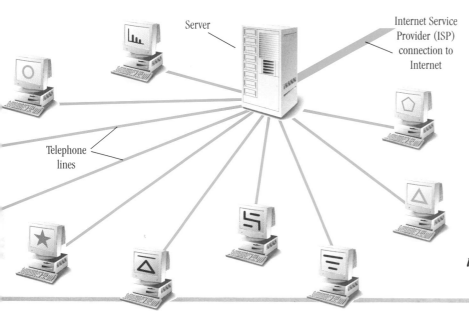

Server

Internet Service Provider (ISP) connection to Internet

Telephone lines

◄ *A network is a group of computers that is linked together. Each terminal has a keyboard and screen, but a central computer processes information and links terminals together. Networked machines may be local or far apart. Travel agencies often use this type of network, using terminals to request and receive information. The Internet is a network in which no single machine has control. Instead, many server computers are linked together.*

World Wide Web

The World Wide Web continues to grow in size and importance. What exactly is the Web? How did it start, and what does the future hold?

▲ *Tim Berners Lee, of Switzerland's CERN laboratory, is thought of as the brains behind the World Wide Web.*

A Home Page acts like a book's contents page. This is the U.S. space agency NASA's 'home' page

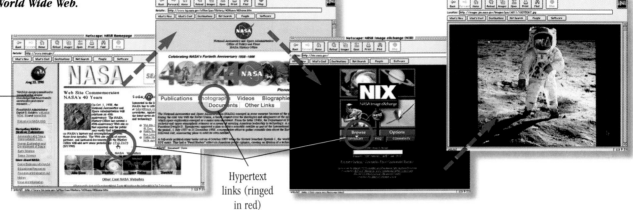

Hypertext links (ringed in red)

▲ *These Web pages show hypertext links. Click on an underlined word and you are taken to another site that has related information. This might be on the same computer or another one, anywhere on the Web.*

The World Wide Web, also known as the 'Web', uses the Internet to let you find information stored in any computer linked to the network. In theory, you can look at anything on the Web. Its success, however, is beginning to create its own problems. For example, tight security may be necessary to protect people using credit cards on the Web.

On the Web, you see information on a computer screen as electronic 'pages'. To change pages, you click on an on-screen 'hotlink.' The hotlink is a key part of the Web. It uses a computer program called 'hypertext'. Clicking on the hotlink (also called a hyperlink) takes you off to another related Web page.

This system has roots in 1945, with the work done by U.S. scientist Vannevar Bush, who was one of the first to predict the information explosion. Bush proposed using a 'memex,' a machine that not only stored information, but could also lay a trail of related words and pictures. The memex was never built, but in 1960, programmer Ted Nelson was inspired by the idea to write the hypertext computer language. This used hyperlinks to take a user on a trail of linked information sources.

▲ *Vannevar Bush is often called the 'father of the information age', as he saw in the 1940s how important access to information would be in the future.*

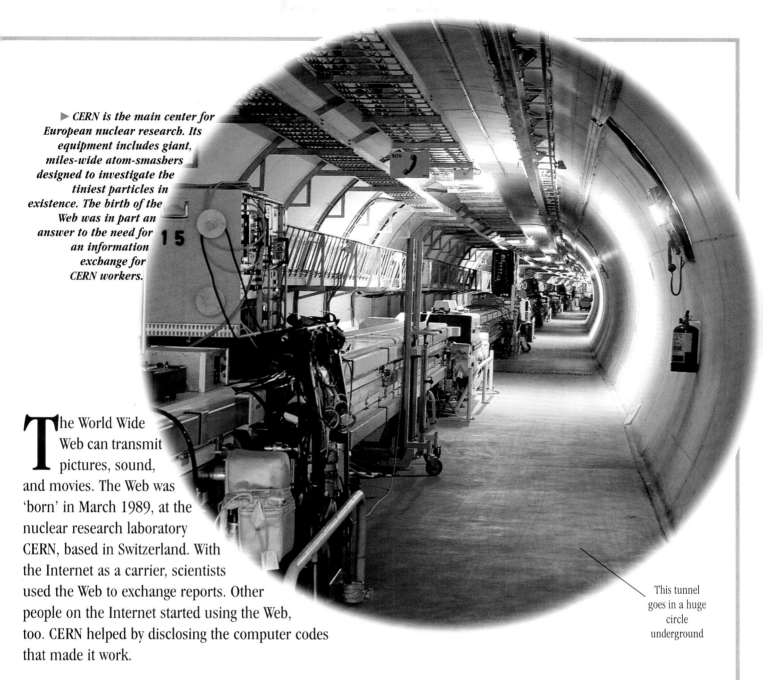

► CERN is the main center for European nuclear research. Its equipment includes giant, miles-wide atom-smashers designed to investigate the tiniest particles in existence. The birth of the Web was in part an answer to the need for an information exchange for CERN workers.

This tunnel goes in a huge circle underground

The World Wide Web can transmit pictures, sound, and movies. The Web was 'born' in March 1989, at the nuclear research laboratory CERN, based in Switzerland. With the Internet as a carrier, scientists used the Web to exchange reports. Other people on the Internet started using the Web, too. CERN helped by disclosing the computer codes that made it work.

► You can find something to read on the Web in whatever language you speak. Many newspapers have electronic editions to keep Web visitors in touch with the latest news.

The Web grew with great speed. In less than ten years, it became one of the most powerful information tools ever invented. By 1994, growth was about one percent a day. The numbers of computers being connected ('online') doubled every ten weeks! The use of other Net features grew as well. In 1997, about 2.7 trillion electronic mail messages were transmitted.

Today, the Web has become a useful tool for anyone needing information quickly. Whether it is a scientist seeking the latest research results or someone looking for a travel deal, they will almost certainly find it out there in cyberspace.

Cyberspace surfing

Surfing the Web means being online, or hooked up to the World Wide Web, while moving from one site to another. It sounds fast, but can be more like the 'world wide wait' if too many other people are also using the sites you are surfing.

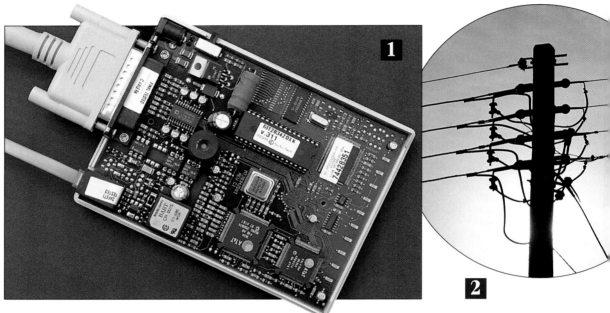

Despite any delays, the technology that joins millions of computers together is almost like electronic magic. What happens as a result of a few mouse clicks is a miracle of technology. Apart from the software in your computer, the first item in the chain that connects you to the Internet is a modem, which stands for modulator/demodulator. The modem's purpose is to connect two computers by telephone line.

1 A signal is sent out by modem after it has been switched on by instructions from a personal computer.
2 The modem converts signals into a form that can be sent down the telephone line.

??? What is a website?

A website is the basic way of displaying information on the World Wide Web. A typical site consists of a number of electronic pages, complete with text, graphics, pictures, and sometimes sound and video, too.

A site's 'home page' is much like the contents page of a book. Instead of turning pages to move around, you click with your mouse on hyperlinks which take you to the other electronic pages on the site.

With each page change, your home computer has to request and receive information from the website. Once the fresh material is 'downloaded' to your computer, you can read it there and then, or you can copy it for later reading or reference.

The modulator converts computer signals into audio signals. The demodulator does the opposite. These signals pass through the telephone line and enable your computer to 'handshake,' or link, with the powerful server computer that sits at your Internet service provider, or ISP. Once the two systems are connected, the ISP's server computer connects you to the Internet. The server is joined to the Internet 24 hours a day, so you can 'log on' any time you like.

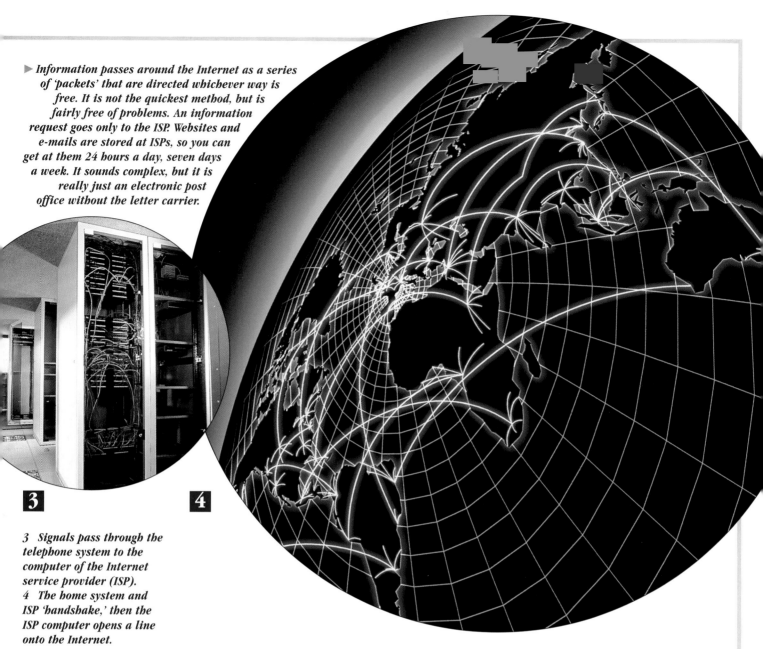

▶ *Information passes around the Internet as a series of 'packets' that are directed whichever way is free. It is not the quickest method, but is fairly free of problems. An information request goes only to the ISP. Websites and e-mails are stored at ISPs, so you can get at them 24 hours a day, seven days a week. It sounds complex, but it is really just an electronic post office without the letter carrier.*

3 **4**

3 Signals pass through the telephone system to the computer of the Internet service provider (ISP).
4 The home system and ISP 'handshake,' then the ISP computer opens a line onto the Internet.

O nce on the Internet, you can send and receive e-mail, join news groups, and use many other services. For most people, the Internet is used mainly for the World Wide Web, and for this you need a 'browser' program. A browser lets you type in a website address directly, or use a 'search engine.'

Search engines are the information seekers of cyberspace. You can type in a subject request, and a search engine comes up with a menu of sites that are related to your request.

▶ *Search engines are index programs that hunt down subjects and sites if you give them details of the subject you want. They range from big international engines to smaller ones that deal with sites in particular countries. There are more than 300 of them.*

Virtual reality

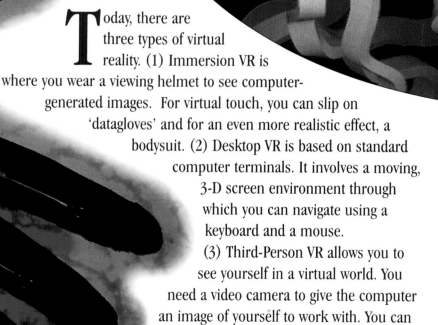

▲ Early developers of virtual reality, Ivan Sutherland (left) and David Evans.

▼ A dataglove is lined with sensors that allow the wearer to 'touch' and 'feel' objects in a virtual environment as if they were real.

Virtual reality is another cyber-technology. It is the science of creating an artificial environment with powerful computer systems.

Virtual reality, or VR, has its origins in the 1965 work of U.S. researcher Ivan Sutherland. He said that a television screen was a window through which you see a virtual or 'almost real' world. Sutherland's challenge was for researchers to make that world "look, behave, sound, and even feel real." This concept did not sound too difficult, but in practice it took until the 1990s before the technology for virtual reality was developed.

Today, there are three types of virtual reality. (1) Immersion VR is where you wear a viewing helmet to see computer-generated images. For virtual touch, you can slip on 'datagloves' and for an even more realistic effect, a bodysuit. (2) Desktop VR is based on standard computer terminals. It involves a moving, 3-D screen environment through which you can navigate using a keyboard and a mouse. (3) Third-Person VR allows you to see yourself in a virtual world. You need a video camera to give the computer an image of yourself to work with. You can play simple virtual games and sports.

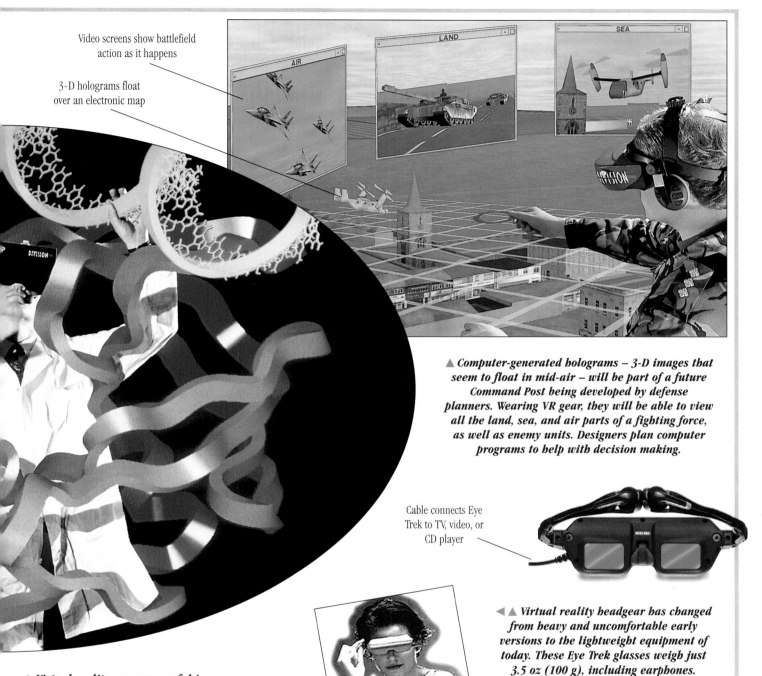

Video screens show battlefield
action as it happens

3-D holograms float
over an electronic map

▲ *Computer-generated holograms – 3-D images that
seem to float in mid-air – will be part of a future
Command Post being developed by defense
planners. Wearing VR gear, they will be able to view
all the land, sea, and air parts of a fighting force,
as well as enemy units. Designers plan computer
programs to help with decision making.*

Cable connects Eye
Trek to TV, video, or
CD player

◀ ▲ *Virtual reality headgear has changed
from heavy and uncomfortable early
versions to the lightweight equipment of
today. These Eye Trek glasses weigh just
3.5 oz (100 g), including earphones.
Japan Air Lines began distributing them
to its jet passengers in 1998.*

▲ *Virtual reality can very useful in
research. This computer simulation
shows the sort of view employed by
a user to visualize a complex
molecule. It can be much easier to
understand something if you can
'see' it as well as look at the
mathematical formula.*

Immersion VR demands a great deal from computers. To get a smooth-
flowing, 'real-time' experience you need a lot of computer processing
power. Any delay in image movement spoils the illusion. It can also give
you 'simulator sickness,' the dizzy effect when your sense of balance says one
thing, and your eyes another.

Desktop VR is becoming popular, especially in the business world. Some
travel agencies have experimented with VR-brochures, so that you can look
around a vacation spot before deciding to go.

Cyber surgeons

Virtual reality has been used in medicine to save lives. Computer technology has allowed doctors to perform operations using cyberspace that really save people's lives.

A new age of medicine began in 1997, when a surgeon in Italy carried out a minor operation. What made the operation different was that the patient was in a hospital in Lisbon, Portugal, roughly 1000 miles (1600 km) away.

This was the world's first 'telesurgery' operation. The surgeon used cyberspace to link with a needle-equipped robot arm. Video cameras were used to keep an eye on the patient.

Cyber-assisted surgical equipment can be more precise than a human surgeon

▲ A surgeon with a computer-controlled robot arm which is inside a model of a human skull. Virtual images are shown on screen. The system can be used to identify tumors, which can be removed without doing too much damage to surrounding brain tissue.

The $150,000 robot arm used in the telesurgery operation is thought to be more accurate and steady than a human surgeon's hand. The metal and plastic machine has a shoulder, elbow, wrist, and hand, plus special sensors that stop it pushing too hard against the patient's skin or organs. The robot's accuracy has a big benefit – the incisions it makes can be much smaller than those required by a human surgeon.

The experts, who may be far away, can help people and provide emergency services in remote areas. Telesurgery operations mean that staff looking after a patient do not have to be specialists.

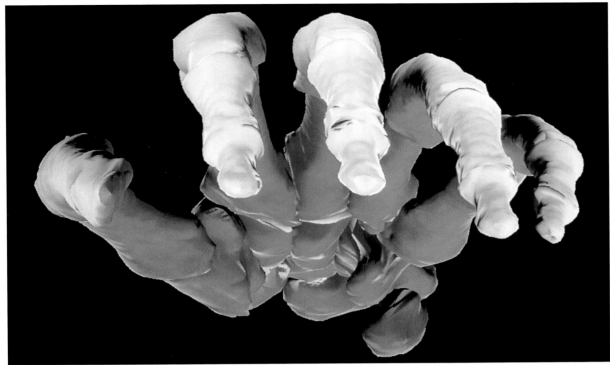

◄ *This ghostly image is a 3-D contour map of a human hand. It shows the structure of the bones beneath the skin and can be used by doctors to see problems not otherwise visible.*

C osmetic surgery is another area where cyberspace could be used in the future. The Virtuoso camera system uses six lenses, which enable a computer to create a 3-D image of a patient's body part, such as a nose. The surgeon can then reshape the 'virtual nose' onscreen until the patient is happy with the new look. The real surgery can take place later.

One leading plastic surgeon predicted virtual reality will be central to plastic surgery of the future. He said that before long, plastic surgeons will practice on VR machines before they are allowed to work on real patients, just like aircraft pilots use flight simulators.

Egg-shaped Virtuoso camera, designed for accurate 3-D imaging

Can doctors use the World Wide Web for operations?

The answer is yes. Cyberspace came into its own early in 1998, when doctors working in Manchester, Britain, used it to deal with a complicated leg injury.

To save time, the medical team took instant digital-camera photos of the patient's leg and placed them on the hospital's website. A specialist sitting at home checked the images and made a diagnosis.

It took just 10 minutes for the pictures to be put on the website, and another minute or so for the specialist to view them and give instructions. The scheme worked well, and the operation was successful.

However, delicate remote-control operations need special links that will not get broken or interrupted.

▼ *Virtual reality meets eye surgery. A U.S. student practices with a headset and joystick control. An advantage of the VR system is that the operation can be viewed from any angle, including angles that would not be possible with a live patient.*

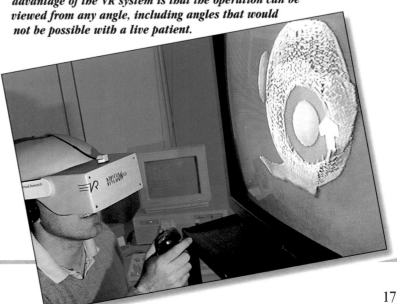

VR universe

▲ *Blurred television pictures were the best that electronics could provide for the first humans landing on the Moon in 1969. Here you can just make out Neil Armstrong's helmet, with the spacecraft ladder behind. High quality photographs were taken later with film cameras.*

S pace scientists and mission planners say cyberspace technology allows them to explore space without leaving the comfort of Earth.

Back in the 1960s, U.S. space researchers worked successfully to put humans on the Moon. It was an expensive mission, driven mostly by politics. At the time, there was a 'space race' between the U.S. and the USSR. By the 1990s, things had changed, and now a major concern of space exploration is to do things cheaply as well as quickly.

▶ *VR helps astronauts train for life on the future International Space Station.*

▲ *You may be able to drive this moon rover from Earth in the future. It is equipped with cameras for a virtual reality view of the Moon.*

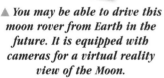

Websites in space?

In cyberspace, our own planet Earth is no longer the only address for telecommunications.

In 1998, Web experts were predicting that to allow for cyber-connections in space exploration, it will be necessary to add an extra word to all electronic addresses.

The experts assume there will be space colonies on other planets in the future. With this in mind, they have suggested that a Web address on this planet ends in 'earth' Addresses on other worlds would end in '.mars' '.moon' and so on.

N ASA's Pathfinder mission, which landed a small rover vehicle on the surface of Mars in 1997, marked the beginning of an era of low-cost cyber-explorations. This space trip took just 38 months from concept to touchdown, had fewer than 300 people on the team and cost about $250 million. Compare this with the $1.5 billion and 1000-plus staff needed for the two Viking lander missions to Mars back in the 1970s.

In contrast to expensive space flights with human crews, missions such as Pathfinder are far more affordable. A single Space Shuttle flight costs around $350 million, and the proposed International Space Station is expected to cost more than $20 billion.

A further bonus for Pathfinder watchers was that no sooner were pictures from Mars received than they were posted on the World Wide Web. Seeing pictures of another world, as if you were there – 'telepresence' – was simply a matter of getting online for the latest news.

Scientists are now developing microprobes no bigger than a shoebox. These will allow future space flights to include a number of tiny 'cyberships' flying in formation. If one fails, the others will take over. There could be a whole squadron of landers, flyers, and crawlers for planetary exploration. Through cyberspace, everyone on the Web will be able to share the information being sent back to Earth.

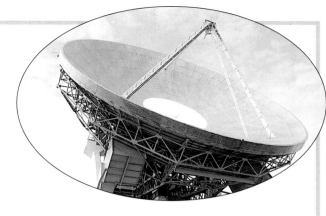

▲ *The normal equipment used for communicating with far-flung spacecraft is a giant, steerable radio antenna.*

Cargo carried in forward section

▶ *Future shuttle spacecraft such as this one, are unlikely to have human crews. Flight control will be either fully automatic or a virtual reality operation. It is likely to be a mixture of both, with teleoperators on Earth taking over from computers only when a change of flight plan is needed.*

Plug nozzles replace traditional rocket engines

UNITED STATES

Twin fins for steering in atmosphere

I magine an astronomy class in the year 2020. Using the Web, you might swoop through the canyons of Mars or check out hurricane winds blasting through Jupiter's swirling Red Spot. As for missions with crews, breakthroughs in space technology will one day allow humans to explore the Solar System and stars beyond. For now, cyberships are far cheaper, and safer.

▶ *The Red Spot (arrowed) is a hurricane in the atmosphere of the giant planet Jupiter. It is like no storm on Earth. It has lasted several centuries. The Red Spot is big enough to swallow our small planet several times over.*

CGI graphics

Computer generated images, or CGI for short, are at the heart of cyber-design for the world of arts and entertainment.

▲ Part of an early-1980s rendering of a 3-D image. The computer instructions took a group of programmers about five years to write!

CGI began in the 1970s, with computers that could create 'wireframes' of objects. A wireframe is like an outline drawing of a scene or object. Adding lifelike texture and color uses a lot of computer memory and is a slower process, as the computer has to work out each separate stage.

Cartoon characters can be created using a desktop computer

▶ The graphics tablet, which combines a touch-sensitive pad with an electronic pen, lets traditional artists try out electronic art.

Throughout the 1970s and 1980s, computer power increased by leaps and bounds. This, together with cheaper equipment, turned CGI into a popular design tool. On a typical desktop computer, the best you could do in the early 1980s was to produce a simple drawing. By the 1990s, the invention of the graphics tablet and complex graphics programs made it possible to create fantastic works of electronic art.

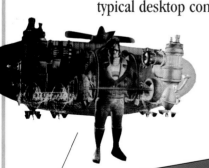

Detailed computer rendering is typical of the best game design

Today, CGI uses 3-D modeling, a type of computer program that helps designers create 'models' that can be animated, scaled, colored, and textured. The computer games industry is a user of such 3-D graphics, with visuals that range from killer robots to cartoon animals. Many ideas still come from nature and the real world. In the puzzle game Riven, many textures were based on landscape photographs of Santa Fe, New Mexico.

One of the images from the puzzle game 'Riven'

Sci-fi scenes can be made easily in a program such as 'Bryce'

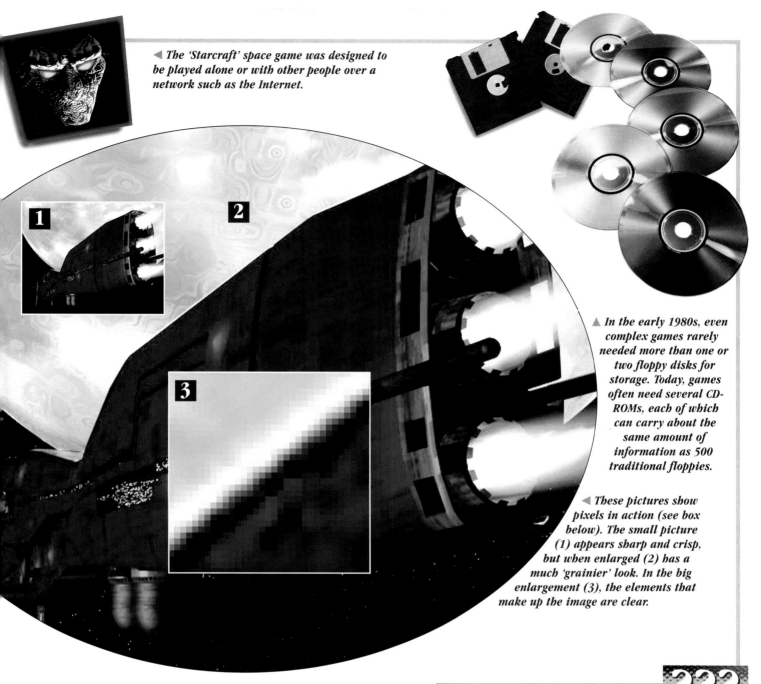

◀ The 'Starcraft' space game was designed to be played alone or with other people over a network such as the Internet.

▲ In the early 1980s, even complex games rarely needed more than one or two floppy disks for storage. Today, games often need several CD-ROMs, each of which can carry about the same amount of information as 500 traditional floppies.

◀ These pictures show pixels in action (see box below). The small picture (1) appears sharp and crisp, but when enlarged (2) has a much 'grainier' look. In the big enlargement (3), the elements that make up the image are clear.

In cartooning, CGI has replaced many human artists. Before computers, teams of cartoon artists, or animators, used to work away, producing all the frames of a cartoon by hand. Even a ten-minute cartoon required nearly 15,000 frames! With CGI, only a few 'key' frames, typically the beginning, middle, and end, from each sequence need to be created by hand. CGI computers can produce all the in-between frames.

The same is true for coloring. Once the key frames are worked out, a graphics program does the hard work. It may sound as if human animators have no future, but since computers make cartoons cheaper to produce, the result has been a boost for cartooning.

What is a pixel?

Pixel is short for 'picture cell.' A computer screen image is divided up into a grid pattern, or matrix, of these tiny picture cells.

The more pixels there are in an image, the more detail an image has. Images with more pixels also need more computer power to process the image, both when it is being created and, later, when it is being displayed on screen.

Many computer games have finely drawn still images. For fast game play, the pictures have much less detail, so they have a more 'blocky' look.

Digital cameras capture images as a pixel grid, and the more expensive models usually give a more detailed picture. 'Megapixel' cameras can provide an image of more than a million pixels.

Digital movies

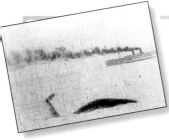

▲ *A prehistoric sea creature stares at a steamboat in the 1925 movie 'The Lost World.'*

The spectacular effects used in most of today's blockbuster movies would not be possible without the cyber connection.

Up to half of a big movie's budget may be spent on special effects, or 'SFX.' Fooling the public with visual tricks is not new. It goes back to the early days of movie making.

▲ *Cyberspace motorbikes, named 'light cycles,' hurtle across a wireframe electronic landscape in the 1982 movie 'Tron.'*

Stop-motion was one early film technique. In the 1925 movie The Lost World, dinosaurs battled each other in (for the time) a realistic way. The dinosaurs were really models that were moved slightly each time a frame of film was exposed.

▲ *The creature star of 'The Beast from 20,000 Fathoms' was a detailed model, shown here stomping through a miniature city. Today, models are still used, along with CGI and real-life camerawork.*

When projected onto a movie screen at the normal speed of 24 frames per second, an illusion of movement was created. Methods such as these were normal for movie-makers until the early 1980s. It was then that digital effects began to revolutionize the movie world.

◄ *The 'Jurassic Park' movies used computer-generated mist, fog, and damp reflections to make the scenes realistic.*

► *'Terminator 2' used CGI equipment worth $3.5 million.*

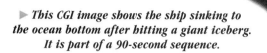
◄ The movie 'Titanic' included an almost lifesize ship as well as many CGI effects. Paintings (far left) helped visualize scenes before shooting began.

Hull sinks below waterline

► This CGI image shows the ship sinking to the ocean bottom after hitting a giant iceberg. It is part of a 90-second sequence.

T he first big-budget movie using computer graphics was Tron, made by Disney in 1982. It featured an electronic world inside a computer. Although the film was not a major box-office success, it was a sign of SFX things to come.

Several movies since Tron stand out for achieving new heights of virtual realism. Terminator 2 (1991) blended live actors and shape-changing robots. Jurassic Park (1993) featured digital dinosaurs with slight speed-blurs to make them look more real. In 1997, Titanic added a further technique, called 'virtual actors.' The film's makers added to the realism of model scenes by showing lots of CGI people, including the ship's captain, moving about on the decks of the doomed ship.

▲ Industrial Light & Magic is one of the top CGI studios. An editor finishes off scenes from the movie 'Return of the Jedi.'

The next aim for movie digital effects is to make virtual movie stars. This idea makes a lot of sense for the studios, as they would avoid paying huge fees to 'big name' actors. However, acting is a lot more than just realistic looks, so virtual actors are likely to be cast in minor roles at first.

Is CGI a quick operation?

The answer depends on the job. The image captured on a single frame of movie film requires a lot of computer memory when held as digital information.

When the CGI work itself is done, the computers carry on working to 'render,' or draw, the screen images and save them to memory.

In the Disney cartoon 'A Bug's Life,' each frame of film took about three hours to render. At 24 frames per second and a movie length of around 90 minutes, that is about 44 years of computer time! A lot of machines had to be used for the job.

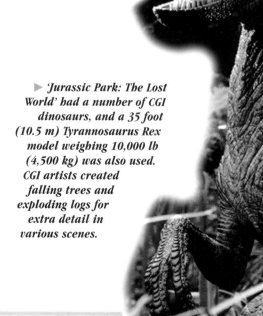
► 'Jurassic Park: The Lost World' had a number of CGI dinosaurs, and a 35 foot (10.5 m) Tyrannosaurus Rex model weighing 10,000 lb (4,500 kg) was also used. CGI artists created falling trees and exploding logs for extra detail in various scenes.

▲ *Groups of concerned people patrol the Web, checking out offensive material and stopping it, where possible.*

The dark side

S o far, this book has looked at many good things about cyberspace, but there is also a dangerous side – the world of 'cyber-criminals' and 'cyber-terrorists.'

For all the benefits of cyberspace, it is proving to be a whole new frontier for lawbreakers, a new 'Wild West' of crime. Cyberspace crimes include cracking, hacking, software piracy, and computer viruses.

▶ *Armed forces use cyberspace to keep ahead of terrorism and other threats. This soldier tests a future system with high-tech communications, night-vision viewer, and advanced weapons.*

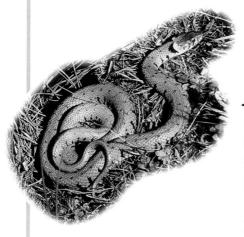

▲ *Crooked offers for making money are to be found on the Web, just like anywhere else. One 'opportunity' was to invest in a snake farm which proved to be non-existent.*

A mateur 'hackers' and professional 'crackers' are people who break through privacy codes on other people's computers. They do it for fun, profit, or politics. Making a website say silly things is the lighter side of a hacker's art. Crackers often do more serious harm, such as breaking into people's bank accounts and secretly putting their money into another account – an electronic bank raid. Cyber-terrorism is a problem, too, with defense establishments and big companies under constant threat for their secrets.

Even e-mail can be used for the wrong reasons. In 1997, a 21-year-old college dropout was arrested for sending 'hatemail' to people he did not like. He sent the 'hatemail' to other students who had better exam grades.

▶ *Many banks and big companies are totally computer-based and make hot targets for cyber-criminals. Cracking a bank's computer codes can leave the bank and its customers at the mercy of such individuals. A power station control system such as the one shown here, can easily be disrupted by cyber-terrorists.*

▲ *The British NAFIS (National Automated Fingerprint Inspection System) was a world first and can compare one million prints a second. With nearly five million prints on file, police can get a result in just a few seconds. NAFIS made its first match in 1997, two hours after being switched on.*

◄ *Crime fighting Robocop-style is already here. While there are no robot police on patrol, digital data systems help the crime fighters track down the law-breakers.*

I t is easy to break the law in cyberspace. Even a simple thing, such as copying words and pictures from a website to your computer, can mean breaking copyright rules. The law is simple: using someone else's material without permission is illegal.

Serious lawbreakers can be caught and stopped. Germany was one of the first countries to let police prosecute people who put offensive material on a website. The Germans say that what is against the law in newspapers, books, radio, or television should not appear in cyberspace either.

Cyber-police work hard to fight serious crime, but with about 300 million computers expected to be connected to the Internet by 2005, they will struggle to keep on top of things.

DARK SIDE DICTIONARY

Encryption Security code written to keep a computer message secret.

Flaming Sending a rude e-mail reply to an unwanted message, such as a spam e-mail.

Software piracy Copying a piece of software without paying for it or having permission to use it.

Spamming Sending advertising e-mail to thousands (or millions) of addresses without being asked.

Virus Program designed to copy itself and spread to other computers. Usually has some unpleasant effect, ranging from an annoying message on screen to total computer failure.

Are there other cyberspace dangers?

These are some of the problems cybersurfers may face:

Bloodshot eyes come from too much screen time. Long periods of staring reduce the eye's natural blink rate, resulting in less eyeball lubrication and sore eyes. Also, eye muscles can get lazy and short-sight may result.

Being alone for long periods is bad, too. Humans need friends, family, good nutrition, and lots of outdoor exercise to stay healthy. The needs of the mind must be balanced with the needs of the body.

Internet links are usually through a local telephone connection. In some countries this is free, in others a charge is made. Too much cybersurfing can be expensive!

Connected world

The electronic tentacles of cyberspace already encircle the world. Even people who do not normally use computers sometimes use cyber-technology.

▲ Digital communications are a part of everyday life for millions of people.

Do you or your family use a computer? E-mail? Mobile phone or beeper? If so, you are in good company. A survey in 1997, showed that seven out of ten people used such cyber items at least once a week. Other questions revealed that these 'connected' people were generally better at their work and more optimistic about the future than ones who were not connected.

◀▲ At left, the Philips 'Doctor Shiva,' named after the four-armed Indian god of wisdom, is a proposed design for a hospital information and communications tool. Above, a future cyber-medical box could give you a medical checkup whenever you want.

If you like gadgets, new ones are exciting, but for people who have 'techno-fear,' an easy-to-use design and product reliability are most important. The Dutch electronics company Philips came up with some helpful ideas in its 1996 Vision of the Future program. The team looked to the future and designed several easy-to-use products. Electricity for many items came from rechargeable batteries, solar cells, or wind-up dynamos, and this cuts down on pollution.

▼ Miniaturized 'palmtop' computers come with Internet software and plug-in modems. They can include word processing, calculating, and graphics functions, too.

▶ Bank, or cash, cards were first used by people withdrawing money from bank machines. 'Smart cards,' which have an IC chip embedded in the plastic, can contain details of medical records, bank accounts, and more.

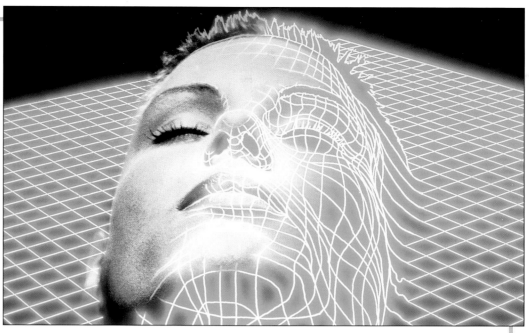

▲ ▶ *A wireframe CGI grids show two uses for cyberspace. At left, a VR simulator used by fighter pilots for combat training. Above, a CGI program can help surgeons remodel a patient whose face was badly burned in a car accident.*

Living patterns changed in the 1990s, with more workers based in home offices. For these people, a home computer is their main tool, but it has other uses, too. Using the Web to get good deals on shopping items, from cars and bikes to insurance and pensions, has become easy and quick.

Thanks to cyberspace, everyday life may be going back to the past, when home deliveries were common. In the future, people will not need to make regular trips to packed supermarkets and shopping-malls. They will choose and order their groceries and supplies over the Internet.

◀ *Mobile phones, first developed in the 1980s, have been shrinking in size and weight. A wristwatch-size videophone could soon be common.*

What is the 'Internet in the Sky'?

'Internet in the Sky' is the motto of the Teledesic corporation, which plans to launch nearly 300 satellites to circle the Earth. The international scheme will provide users on the ground with services such as the Internet and telephone calls. Teledesic wants to sell the satellite system to individuals, schools, and businesses.

Using Teledesic will involve sending a radio or TV signal up into space to the nearest satellite passing overhead. This satellite will then bounce the signal down to rooftop receivers, each about as big as a laptop computer. Millions of people will be able to use Teledesic at the same time, and designers claim that the system will be more than 2000 times as fast as using a standard modem, which is a big bonus for many Internet users.

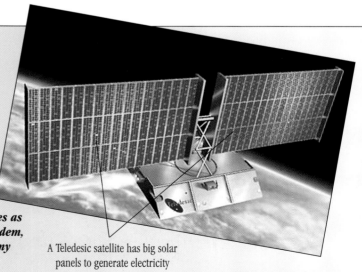

A Teledesic satellite has big solar panels to generate electricity

Time track

T his section looks at important events in the development of long-distance and electronic communications. It features people behind the developments and some exciting possibilities for the future.

▲ *A home computer from 1981, good for the time but technology has since moved on. A late 1990s home computer has 3000 times the computing power.*

2000BC Ancient Greeks use torches and flag signals, especially for military communications.

200BC Carthaginian military leader Hannibal uses smoke signals in battle.

100BC Roman general Julius Caesar uses trumpets for signals in battle.

AD1200 Genghis Khan uses whistling arrows to direct his archers toward enemy targets.

1774 Georges Lesage builds an electric telegraph that sends messages from room to room in his home in Geneva, Switzerland. The drawback of the system is that each letter of the alphabet requires a separate wire.

1794 Claude Chappe builds a military semaphore system in France, using a system of stations. Moveable arms change position according to a code, read by a soldier in the next tower through a telescope. The signal is then passed on to the next station in line. Chappe's system remains in use until the mid 1800s.

1832 The German Baron von Schilling builds a telegraph for Czar Nicholas I of Russia. It connects the Russian capital, St Petersburg, with the Czar's summer palace.

1837 British physicists William Cooke and Charles Wheatstone demonstrate a telegraph system to a railway company. Two years later, they build a 13.5 mile (22 km) line.

1838 Samuel Morse invents the dot-dash Morse code for telegraph messages with his assistant Alfred Vail. The code eventually becomes a world standard for telegraph messages and later for radio transmission. It is still used today.

1851 Reuters news agency begins using the telegraph to send information.

1858 First transatlantic cable laid for telegraph messages between Europe and the U.S.

1862 The U.S. Pony Express message delivery service is put out of business by coast-to-coast telegraph.

1876 Alexander Graham Bell makes the first call on his newly invented telephone. His words (to his assistant) are: "Mr. Watson, come here, I want you." Bell opens a New York-Chicago telephone line in 1892.

1877 U.S. inventor Thomas Alva Edison makes the first phonograph recording, saying the words: "Mary had a little lamb."

1887 German scientist Heinrich Hertz demonstrates the existence of invisible radio waves.

1894 Italian engineer Guglielmo Marconi starts experimenting with radio equipment, transmitting messages about 1.5 miles (2.4 km) in Bologna, Italy.

1898 Magnetic tape recorder invented by the Dane Valdemar Poulson.

1901 Marconi sends a radio signal across the Atlantic, from Britain to Canada, a distance of 2130 miles (3430 km).

1904 First idea for radar by the German Christian Helsmeyer. He suggests transmitting a beam of radio waves, with a receiver to catch reflected energy, like the echo of a person's voice.

1906 First broadcast of music (rather than Morse code) on radio, by American physicist Reginald Fessenden.

1910 Radio used to catch murderer Dr. Crippen, escaping by sea from Britain to Canada. Unknown to Crippen, the ship's radio officer sends daily messages about him – providing headlines in newspapers.

1912 Titanic ocean liner sinks with great loss of life, partly because the radio operator in a nearby ship was off duty and heard no distress calls. After this, all ships have to maintain 24-hour radio watch.

► *Britain's 'Baby' was one of the earliest computers, and the first to use a stored program. It ran for the first time on June 21, 1948.*

1921 First radio station, KDKA of Pittsburgh, U.S.A., goes 'on air.' It is followed a year later by the British Broadcasting Company (now Corporation), the BBC.

1926 John Logie Baird from Scotland devises the first working television system. Despite improvements, the image is fuzzy compared to the Russian-American Vladimir Zworykin's iconoscope. This invention uses electronic scanning, displaying an image on a cathode-ray tube.

1937 First regular TV broadcasts, by the BBC. The system used is based on Zworykin's iconoscope.

1945 British science writer Arthur C. Clarke suggests using space satellites to send radio and TV signals around the world.

1945 U.S. computer pioneer Vannevar Bush says that the future will be an age of information.

1946 U.S. team builds the first digital computer, ENIAC. It is a massive, heavy machine.

1948 Transistor developed by a U.S. three-man team: John Bardeen, Walter Brattain, and William Shockley. It allows electronic devices to be smaller, cheaper, and more reliable than machines that use earlier components.

1953 First workable color TV system adopted by the U.S.

1956 First video recorder developed by a team working for the U.S. Ampex Corporation.

1956 First transatlantic telephone line laid. It allows up to 36 telephone conversations at a time.

1958 U.S. engineer Jack Kilby assembles the first integrated circuit (IC), in which electronic components are put together in one miniature assembly.

1960 U.S. programmer Ted Nelson writes the hypertext computer language. This makes possible a 'hot-linked' trail of related electronic information sites.

1962 Telstar, the world's first communications satellite, is launched. This basketball-shaped device relays live TV signals across the Atlantic Ocean.

1965 Idea of virtual reality first conceived by U.S. researcher Ivan Sutherland.

1969 U.S. Defense Department's ARPAnet project started, with the intention of building an attack-proof military communications system.

1970s Electronic devices using IC chips start to go into general use.

1971 First microcomputers come into use with large corporations and government departments.

1972 American Ray Tomlinson conceives the electronic mail (e-mail) system.

1975 First desktop personal computer developed by IBM Corporation.

1980 Dutch firm Philips and Sony of Japan link up to develop the digital compact disc, which goes on to replace, almost entirely, old-fashioned vinyl discs.

1982 Computer graphics used in the movie Tron.

1984 Apple Macintosh computer uses a 'point-and-click' GUI (Graphical User Interface), designed to make computers easy to use.

1980s Personal computers of all makes start to be used in large and small businesses.

1980s Many universities and corporations develop local-area networks for their computer systems. Many of them link up to other networks. By the late 1980s, networks have grown, and people are using the system for electronic mail between universities.

1984 Canadian science fiction writer William Gibson uses the word 'cyberspace' in his book Neuromancer.

1989 Launch of World Wide Web, a system that allows Internet users to have graphics and sound, as well as text.

1993 Computer-generated dinosaurs are the big-draw stars of the movie Jurassic Park.

1994 Number of people using the Internet on a regular basis passes the 25 million mark.

1990s Personal computers of all makes used in large numbers by people at home.

1997 First telesurgery operation, with a surgeon in Italy operating on a patient in Portugal using cyberspace links.

1997 Remote control robot rover lands on Mars. It is controlled and guided by technicians on Earth via cyberspace links.

1998 World e-mail traffic approaches three trillion messages a year.

The future
Virtual reality equipment enables users to drive a Moon buggy.

300-satellite Teledesic system in low-Earth orbit becomes the 'Internet in the Sky.'

World becomes dependent on the Internet for information and trade.

Internet 2 developed, 1000 times as fast as the old Internet. New system can transmit the contents of a multivolume encyclopedia in one second.

Wristwatch-size videophones come into service, allowing communications anywhere on Earth.

Internets developed for bases on Moon, Mars, and other space habitats.

▲ *A computer-generated image from the 1982 movie 'Tron.' The craft is riding an energy beam.*

▼ *The secret of cyberspace success, the silicon chip is at the heart of all digital devices.*

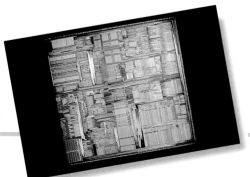

Glossary

An explanation of technical terms and concepts.

ARPAnet
U.S. Defense Department computer network of the 1960s, the forerunner of today's Internet. The name comes from Advanced Research Project Agency.

Browser
Program that acts as a 'window' to the World Wide Web. Through a browser, users can go to a search engine or to websites. Examples of browser programs include Internet Explorer and Netscape Navigator.

CD-ROM
Short for Compact Disc Read Only Memory. Unlike a music CD, a CD-ROM can carry text, pictures, and video as well as sound. The CD-ROM drive in a computer can read any information on the CD-ROM, which is stored in digital form as a spiral of millions of microscopic pits.

CERN
Centre European de Research Nucleaire, an international research base in Switzerland. It is where the World Wide Web originated, initially as a way of sharing research files.

CGI
Computer-generated images. Once confined to hugely expensive computers, CGI is now available for home computers. For big movie blockbusters, CGI special effects are considered essential.

Communications satellite (comsat)
Spacecraft in near-Earth orbit that relays radio and TV signals around the planet. A system of nearly 300 satellites is planned in future as an 'Internet in the Sky' for users of all digital equipment, from telephones to computers.

Cracker
See Hacker.

Cyberspace
The word invented by writer William Gibson in 1984 to describe the universe of electronic communications featured in his books. Today, the word is used for almost everything digital, from the Internet to virtual reality equipment.

Dataglove
Handwear used with virtual reality equipment. The dataglove is fitted with sensitive equipment that lets the user 'feel' images in a computer-generated environment. A bodysuit extends this sense of touch over the whole body. Eyewear lets the user see images in the virtual world.

Digital
Any piece of equipment that operates using the one-and-zero computer information system, in which all information is reduced to a stream of electronic signals. Using a scanner or other piece of equipment, words, pictures, and sounds can be 'digitized,' or converted to a digital form.

Electronic
Describing any equipment that works by adjusting the flow of electrons moving through a circuit, from radios and tape players to computers and televisions.

E-mail
Electronic mail, a system of sending and receiving messages through the Internet. Users who like the speed and ease of e-mail usually refer to envelope-with-a-stamp post as 'snail mail.'

Floppy disk
Magnetic memory disk that is floppy if removed from its 3.5 inch (9 cm) square plastic casing. Now replaced by other types of disc which store more information and which operate quicker.

Graphics tablet
Thin plastic sheet with a touch-sensitive surface. Moving a stylus over it is like using a pen, except that instead of making an ink mark, your movements appear on a computer screen.

Hacker
Amateur who likes to break ('hack') into other people's computer systems, usually through a network such as the Internet. Hackers are sometimes fairly harmless, unlike 'crackers,' who are professional criminals intent on stealing information stored in a computer memory. A cracker may wreck a system or cause equipment that relies on the computer to fail.

▲ ▶ Two examples of CGI graphics. Above, a giant meteor strikes planet Earth in the 1998 movie 'Deep Impact.' Right, wireframe image of the Space Shuttle, 1984.

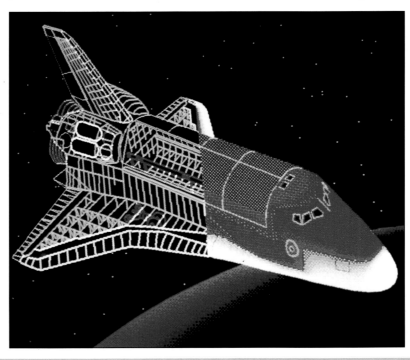

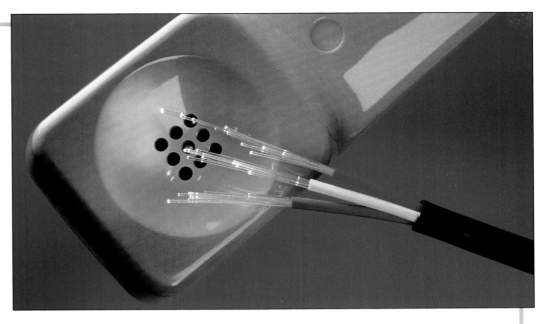

Hologram
Three-dimensional image that appears to float in mid air. Generated by lasers (pencil-thin light beams).

Hotlinks
See Hypertext.

Hypertext
Computer program that allows a user to view a site on the World Wide Web. To go to another Web page, you click on a part of your screen called a 'hotlink'.

Information superhighway
One description of the information passing through the Internet and other networks. Also known as the 'digital highway.'

Integrated circuit (IC)
Electronic circuit that has all parts needed for operation (apart from knobs, buttons and screen) on a tiny chip of silicon. Also known as a 'microchip' for its small size. Used in almost all electronic gadgets.

Internet
A system that links computers all over the world in a large web of digital information that is continuously flowing.

ISP
Internet Service Provider. A company that individual Internet users pay to link them to the Internet. The ISP also acts as a 'post office' for e-mail, holding it for collection and sending it out through the Internet.

Microchip
See Integrated circuit.

Modem
Equipment that converts computer code into a form that can travel on ordinary telephone lines. The process is known as modulation, giving the modem's name, 'modulator-demodulator.'

Morse code
Dot-dash code invented as a signaling system by Samuel Morse in 1838. The letter 'a' is represented as dot-dash; 'b' as dash-dot-dot-dot, and so on for the rest of the alphabet and numbers 1 to 10. In fact, the Morse code is a simple digital system, though very different from the electronic code used by computers.

Network
Any group of computers that are linked together in a way that users can exchange and share information. 'Intranets' are self-contained networks, often used by big companies. A 'LAN' is a local-area network. The Internet is open, meaning that individual computer users or networks can link on whenever they like.

Optical fiber
Ultra-fine plastic tube through which light can pass. Computers can use optical fibers with equipment that changes electronic code to light signals. The big advantage is that an optical fiber can carry at least 10,000 times as much information as a telephone wire.

Pixel
Picture element, one unit of digital information in a CGI image.

Program
A set of instructions that makes a computer work in a particular way. A program may be for calculating, word processing or thousands of other uses. Programs are generally lumped together in the catch-all word 'software.' Equipment needed to use them is the 'hardware.'

Radar
Detection system that sends out radio beams, reading a reflected 'echo' from an object as a blip on a TV screen.

Search engine
World Wide Web software that allows a user to search the Web for information. It works like an electronic telephone book.

Server
Also known as a host, the type of computer used by an ISP to link users with the Internet and World Wide Web.

Telepresence
Remote virtual reality view through cyberspace links.

URL
Uniform Resource Location. Name for a World Wide Web address.

Virtual reality
Literally, 'nearly like real life.' Electronic method of presenting information in a way that seems as real as possible.

Virus
Software program that is designed to attack programs on other computers. Like a virus in a living organism, it can copy itself and spread, hence the name. A virus can do almost anything its creator wants it to. Sometimes the result is a message on screen, sometimes data is completely destroyed. Viruses can be transmitted on the Internet, on memory discs, e-mails, even CD-ROMs. The only answer is a virus detection program, which is designed to search and destroy viruses.

Website
Method of presenting information on the World Wide Web, with a Home Page showing the site's contents. Clicking on hypertext hotlinks takes a user away from the Home Page, to other electronic 'pages' on the website. Sites also often have links to other sites that have additional or related information.

World Wide Web
Electronic network that presents users with text, sounds, graphics, and movies.

▲ *Optical fibers, 'light pipes' that transmit massive amounts of digital information as tiny pulses of light.*

▲ *This military helmet includes a VR 'monocle' which presents information in front of one of the wearer's eyes.*

Index

Acknowledgments
We wish to thank all those individuals and
organizations that have helped us create this
publication.

Photographs and information were supplied by:
Alpha Archive
Apple Computer, Inc/Terry Hefferman
Armstrong Healthcare
Barry Blackman
Blizzard Entertainment
Robert Chase
Corbis
Picture from 'Riven'© Cyan, Inc.
Digital Domain Inc.
Walt Disney Productions
The George Eastman House
Joel Finler
Jane Freund/Visual Interface, Inc.
Grumman Corporation
Klaus Guldbrandsen
Harvard Public Relations
Phillip Hayson
Hewlett Packard
Intel Corporation
JPL Jet Propulsion Laboratory
James King-Holmes/W Industries
KPT Images
Kuwait Airways
Lockheed Advanced Development Company
Hank Morgan
NASA Space Agency
Olympus Optical Co Ltd.
David Parker
Philippe Plailly
Psion Computers
Rosenfeld Images Ltd.
Science Photo Library
Sharp Electronics
Teledesic Corporation
Texas Instruments
TCL Stock Directory
The Stock Market
Geoff Tompkinson

Digital art created by:
Rory McLeish
David Jefferis
Gavin Page
Jon Stuart/Jonatronix
Tom Granberg 'Renderbrandt'